Golf Struggles?

Don Barnes

Published by Don Barnes, 2024.

LifeWorksInThrees.com

Table of Contents

About the Author

Don is the founder and author of Life Works in Threes!™ E-books. He is a lifelong Texan who has traveled extensively while taking a keen interest in human behavior. His curiosity about life and what drives humans led him to the discovery of how life works in threes. He coined this term as the *Tryune Concept.*

Don attended college on an athletic scholarship and then embarked on a 30-year career in the oil and gas industry. Since the year 2000, he has been a consultant for distributors and manufacturers of various industries. Along the way, he worked on his Tryune discovery in hopes of someday sharing his findings with those struggling unnecessarily... in life. What Don surmised from 40+ years of R&D was that people were struggling unnecessarily because they were not aware that "life works in threes." They, for the most part, have been living their lives <u>by chance</u> rather than <u>by choice,</u> he also discovered.

From this, he began focusing on the "mechanics of life" which shows formulas for success with subjects such as *life, health, money, purpose and so forth.* When people are able to grasp the Tryune Concept, they can apply the formulas with topics that interest them and begin eliminating the struggle. This epiphany is what triggered his Tryune venture and is now on the path of sharing with all who desire to improve on their lives.

Don currently resides in Southern California and Texas while overseeing his businesses and investments.

Life Works in Threes™

When I was a kid growing up, no one sat me down and said, "Okay Don, I'm going to show you how life works so that you can navigate your way through adulthood." I graduated from school, got married and went about my way with the "learn as you go" concept. It was kind of like putting together a backyard swing set without a set of instructions. Lots of frustration and do-overs, for sure!

My discovery of the "triune" word and noticing how things come together in threes is really what set me off on researching that maybe "life comes in three" ...sort of a mechanical approach to managing life, if you will. I combed the libraries and bookstores for information on this and found one book on the subject that was written back in 1951. The author's name was John S. Arant.

What Mr. Arant had to say is this "For lack of a better name, I have called this *The Triangle of Triumph* and therefore, consistent with the name, since most of these conclusions are built on the geometric figure of the triangle." He continued "All Life and all lives are seated in, and circumscribed by, the triangle. The Author and Source and Director of all life is Himself triune in character – Father, Son, and Holy Spirit. Man is of triple nature – body, mind, and spirit – and within those three there are many triangles – desires, development, decay; intellect, will, sensibilities. Of this "paced interlude in the midst of eternity" which we call time there is the triangle of Past, Present, and Future. Space – that limitless and measureless element of the physical universe – is best known in terms of Height, Breadth, and Depth. Try building yourself some triangles along the lines of your Will, your Work, your Way – You will find some interesting angles.

So, for the first time, I realized that life is designed in a mechanical way to come in threes. That means you don't have to rely on wishing and hoping things turn out okay. You can actually look at the three parts that a particular thing is made of and then apply them to get what you're wanting. Like a three-ingredient recipe or a combination lock. With a combination lock, you need the three exact numbers to unlock the lock...otherwise you will continue to struggle.

Some 40 years later, I accumulated things that work in threes and that's when I knew I needed to share this with anyone wanting answers. To have success/harmony in your life, just apply the three parts of an area you're working on, and things will fall into place. I also learned that the recipe for success with just about anything is by doing these three things, consistently – THINK positively, SPEAK positively and ACT positively. For example, if I want to be a successful artist. I would think to myself "I can do this because I have the talent." Then I would speak it this way "Yes, I am working on my art degree and plan to do portraits professionally." Finally, I would act on that by taking art classes and continue crafting my skill. Eventually, I will see the positive results/ success I'm looking for.

Conversely, if I think positively but speak negatively...it will cancel out. Or if I speak positively but have no positive action going on...nothing will happen.

I looked up "How Life Works" and "The Mechanics of Life" and these are really talking about the biology of how our cells work and other chemistry. TRYUNE WORKS! teaches that life is kind of like building blocks. Pick a topic you may be struggling with. See the three parts that topic consists of and then start applying them...on a consistent basis. That will help you overcome the struggle and get you back in harmony/ success with how life works.

For 30+ years I was a golf instructor (by accident). My two kids had some success playing junior golf and so friends and neighbors would ask me to show them and their kids how to play golf successfully. From all of this, I got pretty good at watching golfers on the driving range and could spot right away why they were struggling with hitting bad golf shots. I was able to do that because I knew the three steps to hitting good golf shots. I learned them from studying golf and played for several decades. I "broke the code" for me so to speak.

So now you know that life works in threes. You can live your life *by choice* rather than *by chance* and that my friend… is the key to a fulfilling life.

LIFE WORKS
IN THREES!

My sanctuary on the Pacific coast

Introduction

Golf has maintained enduring popularity worldwide for its blend of challenge, precision, and outdoor enjoyment. As a sport that can be played by people of all ages and skill levels, golf offers a unique opportunity for social interaction, exercise, and relaxation. Its appeal spans generations, with courses designed to accommodate varying levels of difficulty, from beginner-friendly layouts to championship-caliber challenges. Beyond its competitive aspect, golf is appreciated for its scenic landscapes and the camaraderie it fosters among players. Whether played casually with friends or professionally in tournaments, golf continues to attract enthusiasts who appreciate its strategic gameplay and the chance to unwind amidst nature's beauty.

According to golf statistics on the internet, there are about 120 million golfers in the world. Of those, 90% shoot scores of 80 – 100+ for a round of golf. 75% shoot scores of 90-100+ and 49% shoot 100+. Less than 5% of golfers in the world shoot in the 70s and the pros are in the 1% category. In essence, you have novice golfers, weekend golfers and pro-type golfers. Novice golfers need to work on basic fundamentals. Weekend golfers need to work on course management. And pro-type golfers focus on tweaking their equipment. They want every little advantage they can get and still play within the rules of golf.

Golf is not just about keeping score. I have played many rounds of golf without keeping score so I could enjoy the scenery and relax. If you're super competitive then keeping score is probably best for your game. If doing some R&R, it's perfectly okay to just hit the ball and enjoy the ride around a golf course. Whatever floats your boat.

My background with golf consists of decades of playing and teaching. My daughter played high school golf and made it to the state regional finals. My son played collegiate golf and was 2x All America for his alma mater. As a family, we've had lots of fun with golf. By reducing golf to just three things necessary to play decently has been a family secret until now.

My discovery of the Tryune Concept

Before we dive into golf struggles and how to overcome them, let me share my discovery of the Tryune Concept and how life works in threes. It all began in the summer of 1982.

I grew up with parents who treated everyone with decency and respect. My three older sisters and I were raised in a home that was "middle-class traditional." We lived in modest homes in different small towns, attended school and church on a regular basis and celebrated all the traditional holidays. Eventually we settled during the spring of 1964 in the big city of Houston, Texas. I'll never forget the vastness of the city and hearing sirens from police cars, fire trucks and ambulances on a regular basis. I was excited and scared at the same time.

Once settled in this fast-paced city, I finished my growing-up years with an academic diploma and sweetheart intact. I got a job, bought a car, got married, bought a house and produced two beautiful babies in a span of about 5 years. Talk about having to grow up fast!

Things went from great in my childhood to absolute misery in my young adulthood. I began to struggle with my job because deep down I just hated what I was doing. This problem created a snowball effect because soon after, my weight, my finances, my relationships, my happiness and everything else worth saving was going down the drain. I eventually hit a level of frustration that I had never experienced before and didn't know how to get out of it. My cry for help was for anyone or anything to come to my rescue. I just ran out of solutions for my situation.

This is when my discovery happened.

One night shortly after my meltdown, while sleeping soundly, the word "triune" began to softly pound in my head like a mantra. I woke up a little startled and decided to go look up the word in my favorite dictionary (this was WAY before Google.) The definition said '**triune** (try-une) – 1) a group of three things; united. 2) Being 3 in 1 such as *humans are mental, physical and spiritual.* I scratched my head, got a glass of water and went back to bed.

The next day while driving around town, I began thinking about things that I was taught in my younger years that came in threes. My Boy Scout manual taught that to have **character**, I needed to be *1) physically strong,* 2) *mentally awake and 3) morally straight.* My high school football coach would say emphatically "If you want to be **a good football player**, you have to be *1) mobile 2) agile and 3) hostile!*" My first sales manager shared with me that to be **a successful salesman**, I needed to have *1) sales skills, 2) product knowledge and 3) a good image.*

"Hmm", I thought, "wonder if there are other examples out there of things that work in threes?" So, some 40 years later, I have researched and discovered that many, many things work in threes. What this message was telling me is that to achieve success or balance in any significant area of my life, the three things that area consisted of had to be present, continuously. That's when I had my epiphany. This discovery was telling me the secret to how life <u>really</u> works...in a mechanical way.

Tryune is a play on the word "triune" as an invitation to "try" this concept. Furthermore, we do not say that life <u>only</u> works in threes. Life also works in ones, twos, fours and so on. What has been observed though is that the many things significant to life, just so happen to come and work in threes. That's what is being shared in this book.

Now, you are about to see 40+ years of research and proof that life works in threes. I did not make up any of these topics. I invite you to research them on the internet to validate what is written here. There are some interesting facts that most of us have never realized...until now.

How Life Works in Threes (around 200 examples)

<u>**LIFE**</u>

Humans consist of *body, mind and soul.*

A human's basic needs are *health, income and provisions.*

A human's basic wants are *comfort, gain and approval.*

Our minds are made up of the *conscious, the subconscious and the unconscious.*

Philosophy explains *the id, the ego and superego.*

Atoms consist of *protons, neutrons and electrons.*

Motion is explained by *three basic laws.*

Science falls under three main branches: *natural, social and formal sciences*

Time is *past, present and future*...at the same time.

Electricity consists of *ohms, amperes and voltage.*

Music's basic elements are *duration, pitch and timbre.*

Democracy is a government *of the people, by the people and for the people.*

U.S. branches of government are *the judicial, the executive and the legislative.*

Armed Forces protect us on *land, air and sea.*

Environmentally, we are asked *to reduce, recycle and re-use.*

The news program gives us *the news, sports and conditions.*

Our days consist of *morning, afternoon and evening.*

Three months in each season of the year

Our main meals are known as *breakfast, lunch and dinner.*

A balanced diet consists of *good proteins, carbohydrates and fats.*

Traditional Family consists of *father, mother, and child(ren)*

<u>SCIENCES</u>

Three major branches of natural science – *(physical, earth/ space and life sciences)*

Three major branches of modern physics - *(classical, relativistic, quantum)*

Three major branches of biology *(botany, zoology, microbiology)*

Three spatial dimensions: *height* (up/down), *width* (left/ right) and *depth* (forwards/backwards)

Three-gauge bosons (photon, gluon, W&Z bosons)

Three types of elementary particles *(leptons, quarks, gauge bosons)*

Three quarks in every proton *(two "up" and one "down")*

Three primary colors of light *(red, green, blue)*

Three color tone properties *(hue, value, chroma)*

Three laws of motion (*Newton's laws*)

Three laws of planetary motion (*Kepler's laws*)

Three layers of the Sun's interior (*core, radiative zone, convective zone*)

Three layers of the Sun's atmosphere (*photosphere, chromosphere, corona*)

Three types of meteorites (*iron, stony iron, stony*)

Three types of galaxy shapes (*elliptical, spiral, irregular*)

Three substances of the universe (*normal matter, 'dark matter', 'dark energy'*)

Three phases of the moon (*new moon, first quarter, full moon*)

Three planetary regions (*temperate, sub-tropical, tropical*)

Three layers of the Earth (*crust, mantle, core*)

Three components of an ecosystem (*producers, consumers, decomposers*)

Three types of rocks (*igneous, sedimentary, metamorphic*)

Three types of fossil fuels (*coal, crude oil, natural gas*)

Three hydrological processes (*evaporation, condensation, precipitation*)

Three basic types of (meteorological) precipitation (*liquid, freezing, frozen*)

Three types of substances *(mono-constituent, multi-constituent, UVCB)*

Three phases of (normal) matter *(solid, liquid, gas)*

Three types of covalent chemical bonds *(single, double and triple bonds)*

Three isotopes of hydrogen *(protium, deuterium, tritium)*

Three atoms in each molecule of water *(two hydrogen atoms and an oxygen atom)*

Three endings to salts *(-ide, -ite, -ate)*

Three requirements for fire *(fuel, oxygen, heat)*

Three nucleotide bases in a genetic codon

Three domains of life *(archaea, bacteria and eukaryotes)*

Three major groups of flowering plants *(monocots, eudicots, magnolids)*

Three major functions that are basic to plant growth and development: *(photosynthesis* [making sugars], *respiration* [metabolizing those sugars], and *transpiration* [water vapor loss]

Three things that the chlorophyll in plants needs for photosynthesis to take place: *(sunlight, carbon dioxide and water)*

Transpiration serves three roles: *(cooling the plant, moving minerals* and *sugars through the plant,* and *maintaining the turgidity pressure* [stiffness] *of the plant's cells)*

Three parts of an insect's body *(head, thorax, abdomen)*

BIOLOGY

Three types of cones in the retina, relating to the three primary colors

Three semi-circular canals in the ear *(lateral, anterior, posterior)*

Three sections in the ear *(outer, middle, inner)*

Three ossicles in the middle ear *(malleus, incus, stapes)*

Three segments to each limb *(proximal, mid, distal)*

Three bones in each arm *(humerus, radius, ulna)*

Three joints in the arm *(shoulder, elbow, wrist)*

Three joints in the leg *(hip, knee, ankle)*

Three joints in the elbow *(humeroulnar, humeroradial, proximal radioulnar)*

Three functional compartments in the knee joint *(the femoropatellar, medial femorotibial* and *lateral femorotibial articulations)*

Three types of fibrous joints *(sutures, gomphoses, syndesmoses)*

Three types of bone in each hand (*carpals, metacarpals, phalanges*)

Three types of bone in each foot (*tarsals, metatarsals, phalanges*)

Three bones (phalanges) in each finger and in each toe (*proximal, intermediate, distal*)

Three layers of skin (*dermis, epidermis, hypodermis*)

Three components of a cell (*cell membrane, nucleus, cytoplasm*)

Three types of blood vessels (*arteries, veins, capillaries*)

Three types of blood cells [*red* (erythrocytes), *white* (leukocytes), *platelets* (thrombocytes)]

Three processes of the intestinal tract (*ingestion, digestion, excretion*)

Three germ layers (*Endoderm, Mesoderm, Ectoderm*)

Three parts of a human tooth (*crown, neck, root*)

Three organs of otolaryngology (*ear, nose, throat*)

Three major body systems (*digestive, circulatory, respiratory*)

Three parts to a neuron: (*soma* [*cell body*], *axon, dendrites*)

Three main parts of the brain (*forebrain, midbrain, hindbrain*)

Three parts of the forebrain *(cerebrum, thalamus, hypothalamus)*

Three parts of the midbrain *(colliculi, tegmentum, cerebral peduncles)*

Three parts of the hindbrain *(cerebellum, pons, medulla)*

Three membranes enclosing the brain *(dura mater, arachnoid, pia mater)*

The brain operates on three levels: *consciously* (for cognitive thought and declarative memory); *subconsciously* (for pre-planned actions and procedural memory); and *unconsciously* (for breathing, heart beating, etc.)

Our conscious mind is fed from three sources: *our senses* (which can be fooled); *our memory* (which is flawed); and *our imagination* (which is inventive)

Three aspects of the human mind *(memory, intellect, will)*

Three parts of the human personality *(id, ego, superego)*

The sum of human capacity consists of three abilities *(thought, word and deed)*

Three times of man *(birth, life, death)*

Three periods of the Gait Cycle *(initial double limb support, single limb support, and terminal double limb support)*

<u>MUSIC</u>

Three types of musical notes *(sharps, flats, naturals)*

Three aspects of a song (*lyrics, melody, rhythm*)

Three types of musical chords (*root, third, fifth*)

MATHEMATICS

Three types of a real number (*positive, negative, zero*)

Three parts to any arithmetic operation: for addition: *augend, addend and sum* - for subtraction: *minuend, subtrahend and difference* - for multiplication: *multiplicand, multiplier and product* - for division: *dividend, divisor and quotient*

Three laws of arithmetic operations (*commutative, associative, distributive*)

Three types of equivalence relation (*reflexivity, symmetry, transitivity*)

Three types of symmetry operations (*translation, rotation, reflection*)

Three geometries (*Euclidean, spherical, hyperbolic*)

The number *3* is the basis of an entire branch of mathematics, called trigonometry (from the Greek *trigonon* "triangle" + *metron* "measure")

Three trigonometric functions (*sine, cosine, tangent*)

Three types of average (*mean, mode, median*)

GRAMMAR

Three logical operators (*AND, OR and NOT*)

Three laws of logic (*identity, noncontradiction, excluded middle*)

Three parts of a logical syllogism (*major premise, minor premise, conclusion*)

Three grammatical parts to a sentence (*subject, verb, complement*)

Three persons in grammar [*1st person* (I/we), *2nd* (you or your), *3rd* (he/she/it/they)]

Three genders in grammar [*masculine* (he/him), *feminine* (she/her), *neuter* (it)]

Three forms of comparison in grammar [*positive, comparative* (more, -er), *superlative* (most, -est)]

Three cases in (English) grammar [*subjective/nominative* (he), *objective/accusative* (him) and *possessive/genitive* (his)]

Three parts of a narrative (*beginning, middle, end*)

Components of an essay (*introduction, body, conclusion*)

Elements of a rhetorical appeal (*ethos, pathos, logos*)

Aspects of a story (*plot, characters, setting*)

<u>RELIGION</u>

The Creator – *omniscient, omnipotent, omnipresent*

Christian God – *Father, Son, Holy Spirit*

Jesus – *The Way, The Truth, The Life*

Ancient Near East- *Qudshu, Astarte, Anat*

Classical Antiquity – Many dieties came in threes

Hinduism – Para Brahman is *Brahma, Visnu, Shiva*

Ancient Celtic Cultures – *many example of triad dieties*

Buddhism – *The three jewels*

Taoism – *The three pure ones*

Islam – *Fear, Hope and Love*

Baha'i - *Intention, Power and Action*

Confucianism – *Benevolence, Wisdom and Courage*

<u>OTHER TRIUNE EXAMPLES</u>

3 Coins in a Fountain

3 Days of the Condor

3 Miles in a League

3 Goals in a Hat Trick

3 Piece Suit

3 Feet in a Yard

3 Books in Lord of the Rings

3 Ring Circus

3 Ships of Christopher Columbus

3 Sheets to the Wind

3 Books in a Trilogy

3 Wheels on a Tricycle

3 Wise Men

3-Legged Race

3 Ring Circus

3-Wheeler

3 Cornered Hat

3 Dimensional

3 Musketeers

3 R's (reading, 'riting, 'rithmatic)

3 Sides of a triangle

3 Races in the Triple Crown (horse racing)

3 Angles in a Triangle

3 Trimesters in a Pregnancy

3 Flavors in Neapolitan Ice Cream

3 Stars in Orion's belt

3 Barleycorns in an Inch

3 Hands on a Clock (with the Seconds Hand)

3 Colors in a Flag

3 Minute Egg

3 Great Pyramids at Giza

3 Holes in a Bowling Ball

3 Colors in a Set of Traffic Lights

3 Minutes in a Boxing Round

3 Teaspoons in a Tablespoon

3 Legs on a Stool

3 Monastic Vows (Obience, Stability, Conversatio Morum)

3 Body Types: Endomorph, Mesomorph, Ectomorph

3 Ring Notebooks

3 Germ layers: Endoderm, Mesoderm, Ectoderm

3 Species of Homo: Homo habilis, Homo erectus, Homo sapiens

3 Basic parts of a camera: Lens, Shutter, Sensor

3 Stages of a Project lifecycle: initiation, planning, execution

The Truth, The Whole Truth and Nothing but the Truth

Life, Liberty and the Pursuit of Happiness

Hear no Evil, See no Evil, Speak no Evil

National motto of France/Haiti: Liberty, Equality, Fraternity

Paper, Rock, Scissors

Ready, Aim, Fire

On Your mark, Get Set, Go

Olympic medals of gold, silver, bronze

Types of joints (ball & socket, hinge, pivot)

Stages of a rocket launch (launch, orbit, re-entry)

Parts of a joke (setup, delivery, punchline)

Primary components of a transistor (emitter, base, collector)

Primary components of an airplane (fuselage, wings, empennage)

Basic components of a computer: CPU, memory, storage

Three phases in the development of technology (*eotechnic* [*mechanical*], *paleotechnic* [*steam-powered*] and *neotechnic* [*electric-powered*]

Communication systems require three components (*transmitter, channel, receiver*)

The list goes on. See if you can find more examples as they are everywhere in our universe. Now that you know that life works in threes (with proof!), we can begin to apply this concept to whatever topics we want.

So, to overcome struggles in golf, we need to apply the three areas that golf consists of – EQUIPMENT, SWING and GAME. Let's get started!

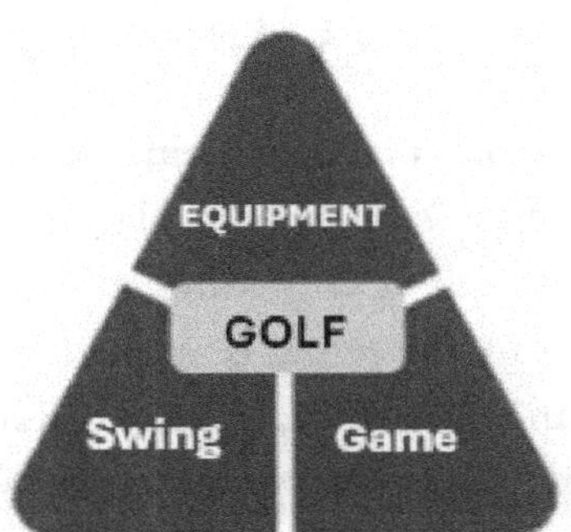
EQUIPMENT
GOLF
Swing
Game

GOLF

In golf, the debate between a learned swing versus a natural swing has long been a topic of discussion among players and instructors alike. While some may seem to have a "natural" talent for the game, many golfers find that mastering the swing is a learned skill that evolves over time with practice and guidance. Every golfer's swing is unique, influenced by factors like body type, flexibility, and coordination. However, even those who appear to have a natural affinity for the sport often benefit from refining their technique through instruction and repetition.

Professional golfers and coaches emphasize the importance of learning and developing consistent, effective swing mechanics through instruction and practice. Techniques such as grip, stance, alignment, and posture are foundational elements that contribute to a successful swing. These fundamentals can be taught and refined through lessons, drills, and feedback from experienced instructors. By focusing on these principles, golfers can improve their consistency and accuracy, regardless of their initial skill level or natural abilities.

Moreover, the mental aspect of golf plays a significant role in shaping a player's swing. Confidence, concentration, and the ability to manage pressure are essential components of a successful swing. Mental training, visualization techniques, and mindfulness practices can help golfers develop a positive mindset and approach each shot with clarity and composure. Ultimately, whether a golfer's swing is considered natural or learned, the journey towards improvement and mastery is a dynamic process that combines physical technique with mental fortitude and dedication to the game.

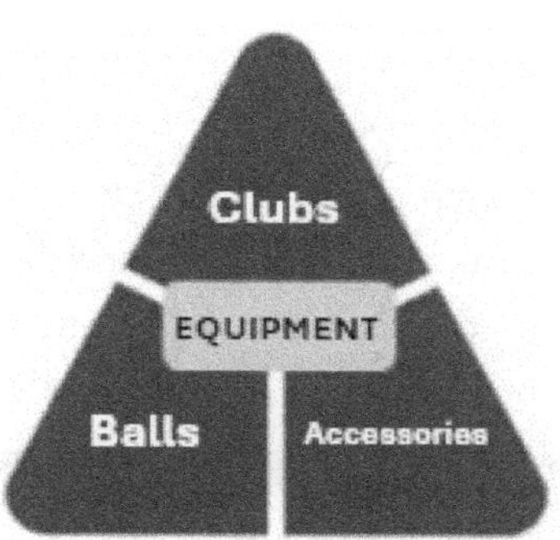
Clubs
EQUIPMENT
Balls
Accessories

EQUIPMENT

Having the right equipment is crucial for enjoying and improving your golf game, whether you're a beginner or a seasoned player. Firstly, golf clubs tailored to your swing and skill level can make a significant difference in your performance. A properly fitted set of clubs ensures that you can maximize distance, accuracy, and consistency with each shot. Golf clubs come in various designs and materials, each influencing ball flight and trajectory, so finding the right ones can enhance your overall experience on the course.

Secondly, golf balls are another essential piece of equipment that impacts your game. Different types of golf balls offer varying levels of spin, distance, and feel. Choosing the right ball for your swing speed and playing conditions can help you optimize your performance and achieve better results on the greens and fairways. Additionally, having enough golf balls in your bag ensures that you can practice without interruption and minimize distractions during your round.

Furthermore, proper golf attire and accessories contribute to comfort and convenience on the course. Wearing comfortable, weather-appropriate clothing allows you to focus on your game without being distracted by discomfort. Additionally, essential accessories like golf gloves, shoes with good traction, a sturdy golf bag, and a reliable rangefinder or GPS device can improve your performance and enjoyment. These items not only enhance your comfort and performance but also contribute to the overall enjoyment of the golfing experience, making each round more enjoyable and successful.

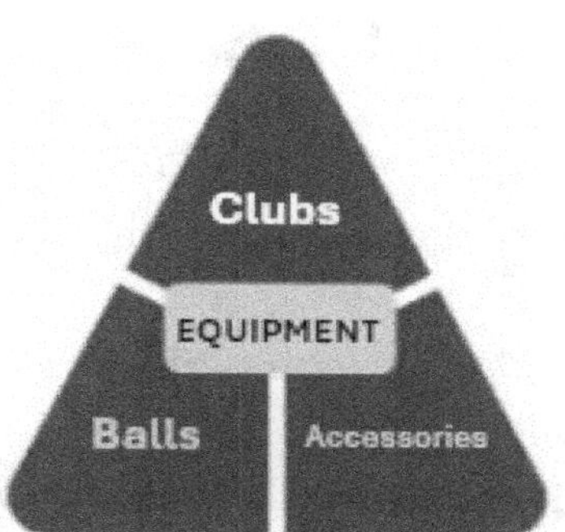
Clubs
EQUIPMENT
Balls
Accessories

Clubs

Golf clubs consist of three parts – *the head, the shaft and the grip.* Depending on your level of play dictates what clubs are best suited for your game.

If you're a novice, then attention to the shaft stiffness is important. Shafts come in lady/senior flex, regular flex and stiff flex for the most part. Using a lady/senior or regular flex makes the most sense for novice golfers because they don't possess the swing speed of a pro-type golfer. Just look on the side of the shaft and you will see symbols like L-flex, Senior-flex, R-flex or S-flex.

If you're a weekend golfer, then you should probably be in the regular or stiff flex shafts. Another key thing would be the lie of your clubhead. This pertains to the irons. Because golfers are of different heights and have different arm lengths, it is sometimes necessary to adjust the lie of the irons. Go to a local pro shop and let them check the lie of your irons and you'll see where you need to be. Lastly, check your grips. You would be amazed at how many golfers play with slick grips or grips that are too small/big for their hands. This affects ball flight so it is important to look at.

The pro-type golfers know how important equipment is as they are constantly checking for ways to tweak their clubheads, shafts and grips. They've mastered the golf swing and course management. The only thing left for improvement is their equipment. Some golfers at this level become club fitters in their garage since they spend so much time on this.

The golf business is a lot like the car business...constantly coming out with new clubs to make more sales. The other thing to mention is that you do not need 14 clubs to play golf. Golf companies offer 14-club sets in hopes that you will spend more. I use eight clubs when I play and here's why. An 8-iron for example can go from 130 -150 yards depending on the swing. Swing softly and it goes shorter. Swing harder and it goes farther. Plus, your golf bag will be lighter and easier to carry.

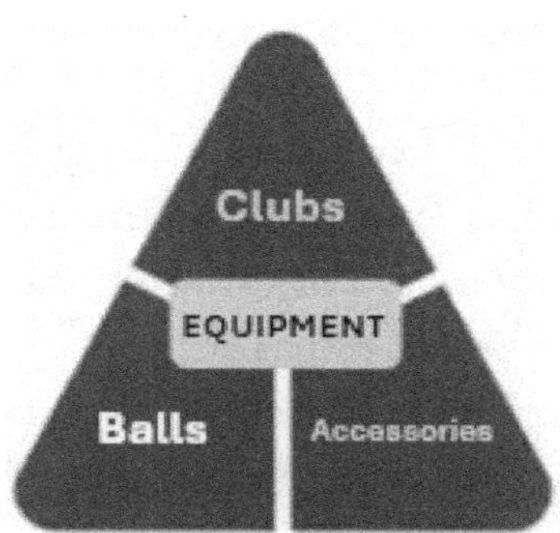
Clubs
EQUIPMENT
Balls
Accessories

Balls

All golf balls are <u>not</u> created equal. There are golf balls that go far but have very little spin. Then you have some that go a good distance plus have some spin. Lastly, you have the pro ball which has much spin and will go far because the pros hit it so hard.

The importance of having spin on the ball is so it will stop when it hits the greens. The balls that have no spin will hit the greens and then bounce right off the back end. Novices play with no-spin golf balls because they go farther and cost less. Novice golfers tend to lose a lot of golf balls in the water or woods. The cheaper ball makes more sense for them.

Weekend golfers typically play with a middle of the road golf ball because it has some spin and is still budget friendly. The golf balls in this range have a "soft" cover while giving the golfer a 50/50 benefit – half for distance and half for spin.

Pro-type golfers hit the most expensive golf balls in golf. They want to be able to "work" the ball. Hitting draws, fades, hooks and slices is part of their game. To do that, you need lots of spin from your golf ball. These pro-type golfers rarely lose golf balls when they play.

As far as brands go, they are all about the same. They have to be to comply with USGA specifications. So, it really comes down to appearance. Which logo do you like and what color ball do you want to play with?

If you're a novice golfer, don't buy brand new balls. Get the second-chance golf balls that are just as good as new at half the price usually. If you're going to lose some balls, you might as well save some money doing it.

For ball tricks such as finding the "center" of the ball or soaking them in salt water...refer to Youtube.com with video showing how and why it is done by the pro-type golfers. Once again, they will do anything to shave a stroke or two off their score.

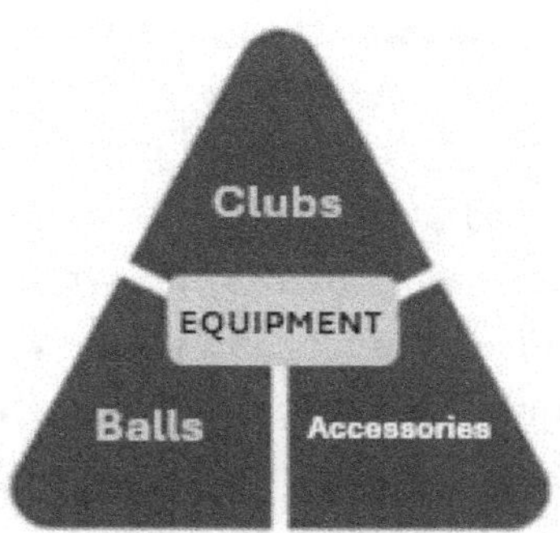
Clubs
EQUIPMENT
Balls
Accessories

Accessories

Let's talk about golf shoes. I have played golf barefooted, with sandals, boots, tennis shoes and street shoes. Trust me when I say...golf shoes really make a difference. Without the cleats/nubs on the soles of golf shoes, you will find yourself slipping and sliding while swinging the club. So, invest in a good pair of supportive golf shoes and your feet will thank you forever.

Here are some more items to bring along:

- Golf glove – you will get blisters without this
- Golf tees
- Divot fixer
- Golf hat
- Water bottle
- Suntan lotion
- Golf towel
- Ball marker

Naturally you can put these in your golf bag. Some extra items to think about would be band aids and a handkerchief. Why handkerchief, you ask? If it starts to rain while you're playing (and hopefully not lightning!), your hands will be slippery on the golf grip. Your clubs will fly right out of your hands. Amazingly, a handkerchief in your hands allows you to grip the club and hang on to it while swinging. It really works!

As your game elevates to pro level, you will accumulate additional accessories such as range finders, GPS watches, launch monitor and so on. Golf has many items for the novice, weekenders and pro-style players. Go online or to your nearest golf shop and check it all out!

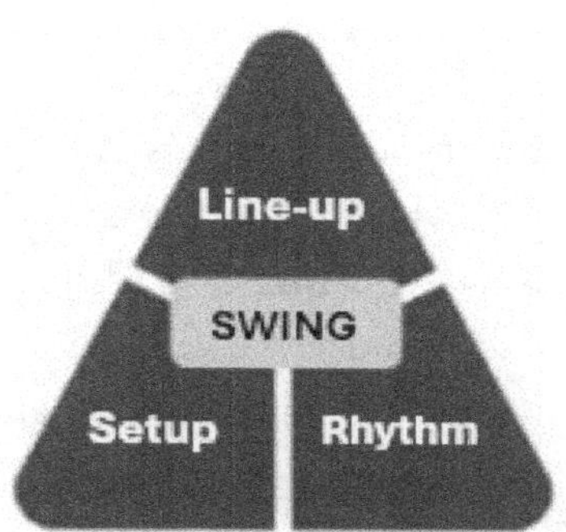
Line-up
SWING
Setup
Rhythm

SWING

In golf, there are various types of swings that players use to achieve similar results—hitting the ball accurately and with distance. One of the most common types is the classic or traditional swing, often taught to beginners and characterized by a full backswing and controlled follow-through. This swing emphasizes rhythm and consistency, aiming to produce straight shots with controlled spin. Many professional golfers, such as Jack Nicklaus and Tiger Woods, have perfected this style through years of practice and refinement, showcasing its effectiveness in competitive play.

Another type of swing is the modern or power swing, which has gained popularity in recent years, especially among younger golfers and those focusing on maximizing distance. This swing typically involves a more aggressive backswing and a faster transition through impact, generating higher clubhead speed and longer shots. Golfers like Rory McIlroy and Brooks Koepka are known for their powerful swings, demonstrating how this style can effectively navigate longer courses and challenging conditions. The modern swing often incorporates advanced techniques in biomechanics and fitness, emphasizing explosive movements to optimize ball flight and distance.

Additionally, there are variations such as the fade and draw swings, which manipulate ball flight through intentional shot-shaping techniques. A fade involves a controlled left-to-right trajectory for right-handed golfers, while a draw produces a right-to-left flight path. These swings rely on adjusting the clubface angle and swing path at impact, providing golfers with strategic options to navigate around obstacles or position shots on the fairway. Both professional and amateur golfers may choose to master these variations based on their playing style and course conditions, highlighting the versatility and creativity inherent in the game of golf. Ultimately, whether using a classic, modern, fade, or draw swing, the goal remains the same—to execute shots with precision, control, and confidence, enhancing the overall enjoyment and competitiveness of the game.

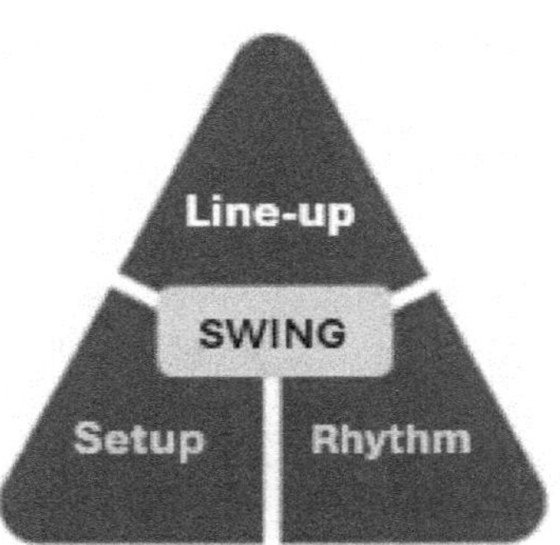
Line-up
SWING
Setup
Rhythm

Line-up

Lining up a golf shot or putt properly before swinging is crucial for achieving accuracy, consistency, and overall success on the course. Firstly, taking the time to align yourself with the target helps set the foundation for a well-executed shot. This includes assessing the distance to the target, considering factors like wind direction and slope of the terrain, and selecting the appropriate club for the shot at hand. By carefully lining up your stance, grip, and body alignment towards the target, you increase the likelihood of striking the ball cleanly and sending it towards your intended destination.

Secondly, proper alignment contributes to maintaining consistency in your golf game. Consistency is key to improving your overall performance and lowering your scores. When you consistently align yourself correctly for each shot, you develop muscle memory and a reliable routine that can be replicated under pressure. This consistency helps you build confidence in your ability to execute shots effectively, whether you're teeing off, approaching the green, or putting.

Lastly, lining up a golf shot before swinging enhances your mental focus and decision-making process on the course. It encourages you to visualize the desired trajectory and landing spot of the ball, fostering a strategic approach to each shot. Taking a moment to line up also allows you to mentally prepare and commit to your shot, reducing the likelihood of indecision or rushed swings that can lead to errors. Overall, by emphasizing the importance of alignment in your golf routine, you improve your ability to control the outcome of each shot and maximize your enjoyment of the game through improved performance and consistency.

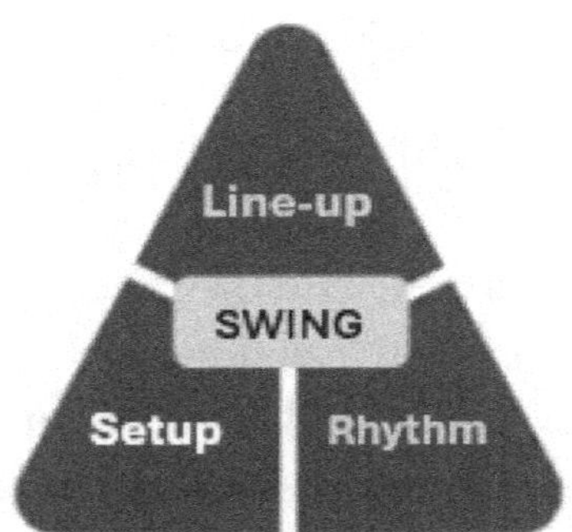
Line-up
SWING
Setup
Rhythm

Setup

This is where golf goes from being a natural swing to being a "learned" swing. The setup sets you up for success or failure in a golf shot because it influences the direction of the golf ball. So, let's go through the process of setting up properly to help your chances of hitting a good shot or putt.

Stepping up to the ball – if a golfer doesn't know better, he/she will walk up to the golf ball on the ground and then set their club down behind the ball. Conversely, what needs to happen is to set the club/putter down behind the ball first, then step up to the ball with a nice poster. Remember – set club down first, then step up to the ball.

Gripping the club – naturally some golfers put a "death grip" on the club before swinging because they want to hit the ball hard. Conversely, you need to grip the club softly (like holding a bird in your hands) to relieve any tension you might have in your upper body. A loose grip promotes flexibility and allows you to swing/putt better.

Poster – a way to vision your poster at setup is like that of a shortstop playing his/her position or like sitting on a stool. You want your arms to hang naturally under your chin and your buttocks sticking out to prevent falling over during your swing. Do not stand straight up or hunch over too much. Just a nice, relaxed poster also promotes a smooth golf swing.

Weight distribution – as you set up with a good poster then think about your weight distribution with back-and-forth weight and side-to-side weight. In your setup, you should be able to wiggle your toes. If not, you have too much weight forward and need to get back on your heels more. Side-to-side, you will have 60% of your weight on the back leg to start and 40% on your front leg. You can do 50/50 here if it's more comfortable for you.

If putting – make sure your eyes are over the ball before you start your putting stroke.

This is basic, fundamental setup. Watch some videos on Youtube.com to get a good look at this.

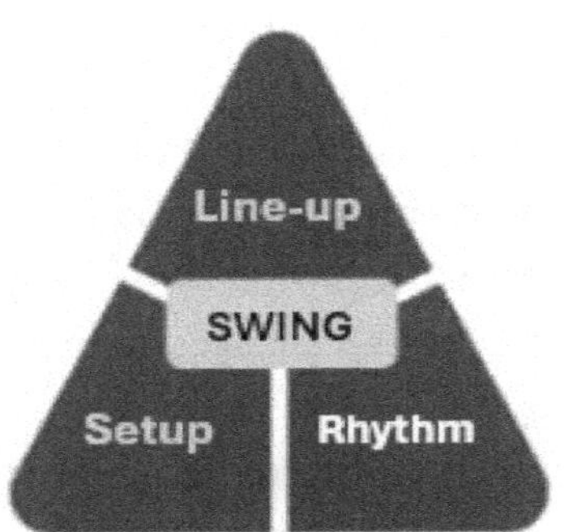

Line-up
SWING
Setup
Rhythm

Rhythm

Maintaining a consistent tempo during a golf swing or putt is essential for achieving accuracy, distance control, and overall success on the course. Firstly, tempo refers to the rhythm and timing of your swing or stroke. A smooth and even tempo helps synchronize your body movements and club or putter through impact, resulting in cleaner contact with the ball. This consistency allows you to develop a reliable and repeatable swing or putting stroke, which is crucial for achieving consistent results from shot to shot.

So, here's to rhythm/tempo I use that works really well. 1-2-3 is the pace of the swing or putt. In your head, whispers this cadence of 1-2-**3!** Start your swing (1) by locking in the elbow of your lead arm. If right-handed golfer, that would be your left arm. Don't squeeze the grip with your left hand...just make your left arm stiff before taking the club back. Now, take your club back slowly (2). No jerking motion and cock your left wrist as you go back. Then on 3, accelerate through the ball! Some golfers "decelerate" at the golf ball and so the shot doesn't go very far. Practice this in your living room or backyard to get the feel for it. It really works well. Remember...1 - 2 – **3!**

The importance of establishing a rhythm/tempo is that your swing will become second nature. When you practice enough, you will get to the point where you're thinking about where you want to hit the golf ball instead of thinking about your swing as you're swinging. Kind of like shooting a basketball. When you jump up in the air to shoot a basketball, you should be focused on the basket, not your shooting mechanics.

This also works for the putting stroke. Start by pushing your grip forward slightly (1), then take it back short and slowly (2) and finally (3!) accelerate through the ball and take your putter to the intended target.

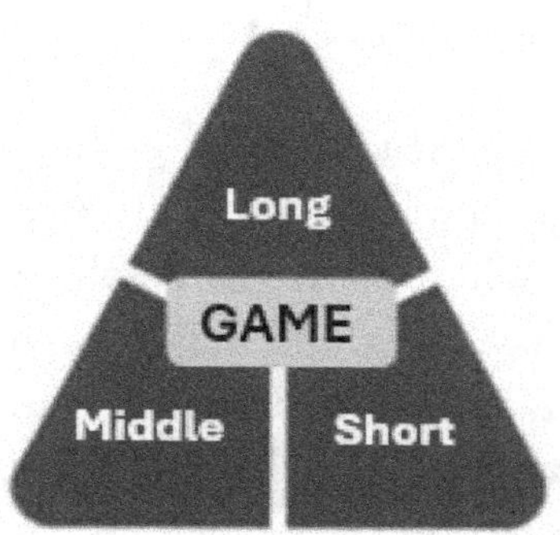
Long
GAME
Middle
Short

GAME

Course management is a vital aspect of playing a successful round of golf, blending strategic thinking with skill execution to navigate the challenges of each hole effectively. Firstly, understanding course management involves assessing the layout of the course, including factors like hole length, hazards, wind direction, and pin placements. By studying these elements before each shot, golfers can make informed decisions about club selection, shot direction, and risk-reward scenarios. This thoughtful approach minimizes mistakes and maximizes opportunities for achieving lower scores.

Secondly, course management encourages golfers to play to their strengths and minimize weaknesses. It involves making strategic decisions based on one's skill level and capabilities, rather than attempting high-risk shots that may lead to trouble. For instance, choosing a safer landing area off the tee or laying up short of a hazard instead of going for a risky shot can often lead to more consistent and reliable outcomes. Effective course management also includes managing mental aspects such as patience, resilience, and adaptability, which are crucial for maintaining focus and composure throughout the round.

Furthermore, course management promotes efficient shot execution and time management on the course. By planning shots in advance and visualizing each play, golfers can streamline their decision-making process and maintain a steady pace of play. This not only enhances the flow of the round but also reduces fatigue and mental strain, allowing golfers to perform at their best from the first hole to the last. Ultimately, mastering course management is about making intelligent choices that optimize your strengths, mitigate risks, and capitalize on scoring opportunities, contributing to a more enjoyable and successful golfing experience.

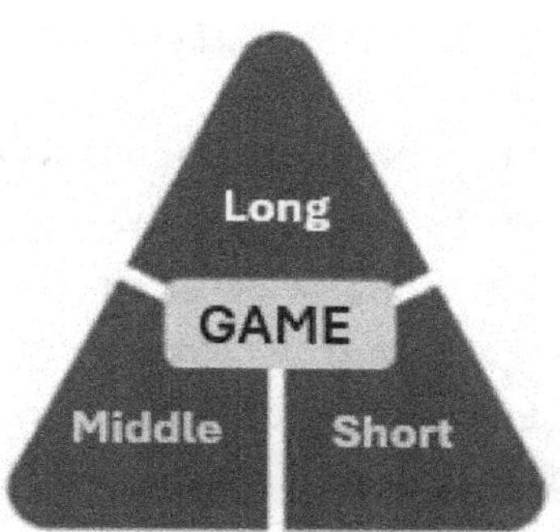

Long
GAME
Middle
Short

Long game

Teeing off in golf presents a unique set of challenges that golfers of all skill levels encounter on the course. Firstly, the pressure of starting a hole with a tee shot can be mentally demanding. Whether you're teeing off on the first hole of a round or facing a crucial shot later in the game, the initial drive sets the tone for the hole ahead. Managing nerves and maintaining focus are essential to executing a successful tee shot, as anxiety or distraction can lead to errant swings and unfavorable outcomes.

Secondly, environmental factors such as wind direction, weather conditions, and terrain can significantly impact tee shots. Adjusting your strategy and club selection based on these variables is crucial for achieving optimal distance and accuracy. A strong headwind may require a more conservative approach, while a tailwind might allow for more aggressive play. Additionally, the positioning of hazards such as bunkers, water hazards, and out-of-bounds areas near the tee box further complicates shot selection, requiring careful consideration to avoid potential penalties and maintain course management.

The technical aspects of the tee shot, such as achieving proper alignment, stance, and swing mechanics, contribute to the challenge. Ensuring a consistent and repeatable motion with the driver or fairway wood is essential for generating power and achieving desired ball flight. Golfers often work on refining their tee shot technique through practice and instruction to improve consistency and reliability. Despite these challenges, mastering the art of teeing off is rewarding, as a well-executed tee shot sets up opportunities for successful approach shots and ultimately contributes to a more enjoyable round of golf.

The driver is the hardest club to hit in the golf bag. If you watch pros and college golfers, they typically use a 3-wood because they want accuracy over distance. Something to think about.

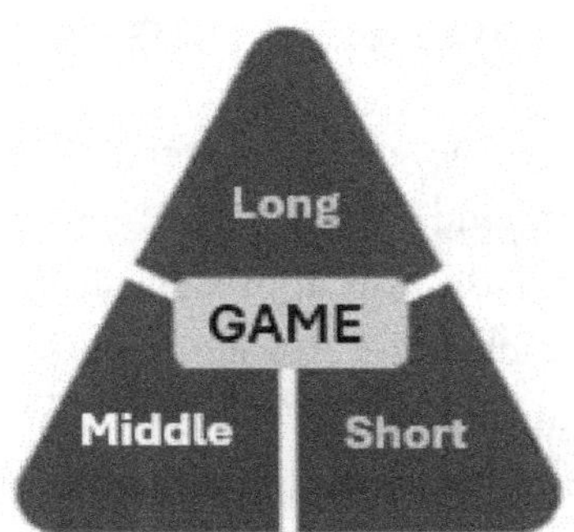

Long
GAME
Middle
Short

Middle game

The approach shot into the greens is a critical phase in every golfer's game, where precision and strategy play pivotal roles in achieving favorable outcomes. Firstly, the approach shot often determines the scoring potential for each hole. A well-executed approach can set up birdie or par opportunities, while a poorly played shot may lead to bogeys or worse. Choosing the right club based on distance to the pin, wind conditions, and potential hazards is essential for optimizing accuracy and control. Golfers must also consider the placement of the pin on the green, as targeting the right area can lead to more manageable putts and increase the likelihood of scoring well.

Secondly, the approach shot requires a balanced blend of skill and decision-making. Golfers must assess their lie, evaluate the lie of the ball, and adjust their strategy accordingly. This may involve considering factors such as whether to go for a more aggressive or conservative approach, depending on the layout of the green and potential risks involved. Additionally, maintaining composure and mental focus during the approach shot is crucial, as it directly influences the outcome of the hole. Visualizing the desired trajectory and landing spot on the green helps golfers commit to their shot and execute with confidence.

Depending on your experience, your approach will be to go for the green or layup. Club selection is the difference between a novice and a weekend golfer...with weekend golfer being the more aggressive. Also, investigate using hybrid clubs for these shots. They are so easy to hit and can help with your score. Long irons are just too tricky sometimes to control.

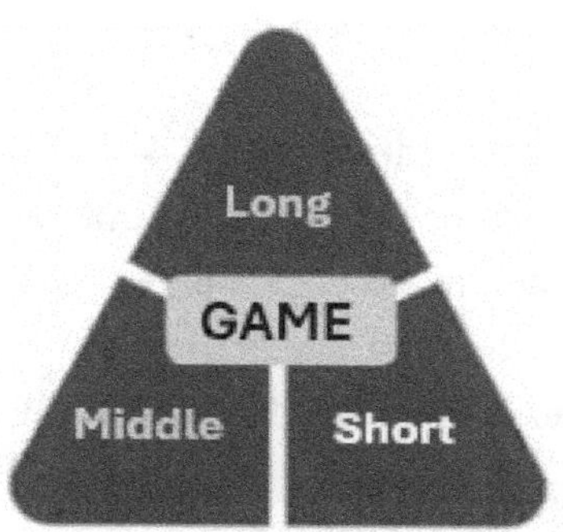
Long
GAME
Middle
Short

Short game

Chipping and putting around the greens are a "touch and feel" thing. That's why it is advised to spend some time practicing these shots. If you watch amateur golfers' warm-up before playing, they will spend most of their time on the range hitting their drivers. Since putting is about 50% of your score, it is better to spend more time on the chipping and putting practice areas.

The short game in golf is often described as the "scoring zone" because it encompasses shots played near or around the green, including chips, pitches, bunker shots, and putts. Mastering the short game is crucial for lowering scores and improving overall performance on the course. Firstly, proficiency in chipping and pitching allows golfers to navigate close-range shots with precision and control. These shots require finesse in judging distance, trajectory, and spin, which can make the difference between saving par or ending up with a higher score. Practicing these skills helps golfers develop confidence in their ability to get the ball closer to the hole from various lies and situations around the green.

Secondly, putting is a cornerstone of the short game and arguably the most critical aspect of scoring in golf. A significant portion of strokes in a round are taken on the putting green, making it essential for golfers to hone their putting skills. Developing a consistent putting stroke, along with reading greens effectively and managing speed, allows golfers to capitalize on scoring opportunities and avoid costly three-putts. Putting proficiency not only enhances a golfer's ability to convert birdie opportunities but also helps them save pars and minimize mistakes. Ultimately, investing time and effort into improving the short game pays dividends by improving overall scores and increasing enjoyment of the game through greater success on the greens.

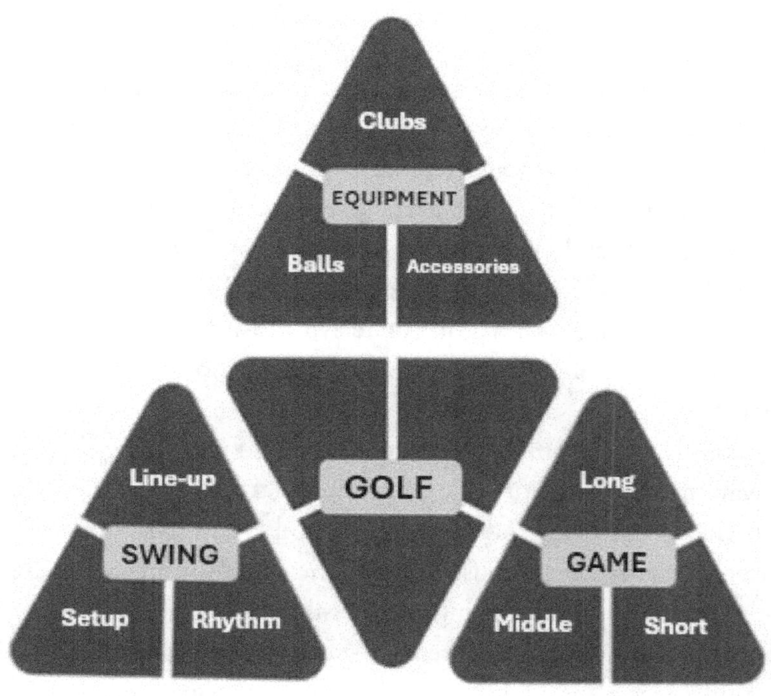
Clubs
EQUIPMENT
Balls
Accessories
Line-up
GOLF
Long
SWING
GAME
Setup
Rhythm
Middle
Short

SUMMARY

Golf is often celebrated as the game of a lifetime, offering unique benefits and enjoyment that span generations. Firstly, golf is a sport that can be played and enjoyed at any age. Unlike many other physical activities, golf allows individuals of all ages to participate together on an equal footing. Whether you're a child learning the fundamentals, a young adult honing your skills, or a senior enjoying leisurely rounds, golf accommodates players at every stage of life. This inclusivity fosters lifelong friendships and bonds, as golfers share experiences and memories across different generations.

Secondly, golf promotes physical health and well-being throughout life. Walking the course provides cardiovascular exercise, while swinging a club engages muscles and improves flexibility and coordination. The low-impact nature of golf also reduces the risk of injury compared to more strenuous sports, making it accessible to individuals of varying fitness levels and abilities. Moreover, spending time outdoors in green spaces enhances mental health and reduces stress, contributing to overall well-being. The combination of physical activity and natural surroundings makes golf a therapeutic and enjoyable pastime that supports a healthy lifestyle over the years.

Furthermore, golf is a sport that challenges the mind as much as the body. Each round presents new strategic decisions and opportunities for problem-solving, stimulating cognitive function and mental acuity. Golfers must assess terrain, weather conditions, and course obstacles, adapting their game plan accordingly. This mental stimulation promotes lifelong learning and personal growth, as golfers continually refine their skills and strategies throughout their golfing journey. Whether playing competitively or recreationally, golf provides intellectual stimulation and a sense of achievement, fostering a lifelong passion for the game and its inherent challenges.

Invitation

From all my years in teaching the game, there were hundreds of students, both kids and adults. I was able to help almost every golfer I taught apart from a handful. The reason I could not help the handful of potential golfers was they did not have *eye-hand coordination*. It would be like trying to teach me to play the piano. I just don't have what it takes to be a pianist.

While golf is for any age, it's not for everybody. If you have played other sports, then chances are you have eye-hand coordination. If not, I'm not sure how you can "get" eye-hand coordination, but it is always worth a try.

The other thing I would mention is not to compare yourself to Tiger Woods or any other pro golfer. All that will do is create frustration during your golf venture. Students from time to time would come to me and say, "All I want to learn is how to hit a 5-wood." and that's what we would work on. Another golfer would request "I just want to break 100." And the most requested comments were executives asking me to help them 'not embarrass' themselves on the first tee box.

Be the individual that you are and work on what interests you in golf. Just hitting your driver better or making more putts or learning how to hit out of trees. The journey from beginner to PGA pro is a long one but the journey to hitting consistent golf shots can be done with just a couple of lessons.

Lastly, I would say, don't get caught up in golf marketing. Dressing nicely and having the latest clubs out won't do much to improve your game. Picking one or two areas at a time and working on that pays dividends. Save your money and have fun playing!

1. Golf Equipment

Here's a list of various types of golf equipment:

1. **Golf Clubs:**
    - **Driver**
    - **Fairway woods**
    - **Hybrids**
    - **Irons (including wedges)**
    - **Putters**
2. **Golf Balls**
3. **Golf Bag**
4. **Golf Tees**
5. **Golf Gloves**
6. **Golf Shoes**
7. **Golf Clothing:**
    - **Polo shirts**
    - **Golf pants/shorts**
    - **Golf skirts (for women)**
    - **Golf hats/visors**
8. **Golf Accessories:**
    - **Golf towels**
    - **Golf umbrellas**
    - **Ball markers**
    - **Divot repair tools**
    - **Range finders/GPS devices**
    - **Scorecards and pencils**
9. **Training Aids:**
    - **Alignment sticks**
    - **Swing trainers**
    - **Putting mats**
10. **Golf Technology:**
    - **Golf simulators**
    - **Swing analysis software/apps**

- ○ **Wearable devices (for swing analysis, shot tracking)**
11. **Miscellaneous:**
    - ○ **Golf carts (electric or push/pull)**
    - ○ **Travel cases/bags for clubs**
    - ○ **Drink coolers**

This list covers the essentials and additional items commonly used by golfers to enhance their game or provide comfort and convenience on the course.

2. Golf Swing/Putting Stroke

A golf swing and a putting stroke each involve several key aspects that contribute to their effectiveness. Here's a breakdown of the different aspects for both:

Golf Swing:

1. **Grip:**
    - How you hold the club influences control and power.

1. **Stance and Alignment:**
    - Positioning of feet, hips, and shoulders relative to the target.
2. **Posture:**
    - Positioning of the body for balance, power, and consistency.
3. **Backswing:**
    - Movement of the club away from the ball, setting up for power and accuracy.
4. **Downswing:**
    - Transition from backswing to impact, generating clubhead speed and control.
5. **Impact:**
    - Moment of contact between clubface and ball, crucial for direction and distance.
6. **Follow-through:**
    - Completion of the swing after impact, influencing accuracy and balance.
7. **Weight Shift:**

- ○ **Transfer of weight from back foot to front foot during the swing.**
8. **Rotation:**
   - ○ **Rotation of the body (hips, shoulders) to generate power and control.**
9. **Clubface Control:**
   - ○ **Alignment and orientation of the clubface at impact, affecting ball flight.**

Putting Stroke:

1. **Grip:**

How you hold the putter affects control and feel.

1. **Stance and Alignment:**

Feet, hips, and shoulders aligned to the target line.

1. **Posture:**

Bent at the waist, eyes over the ball for consistency.

1. **Backswing:**

Short and controlled movement to set up for the putt.

1. **Acceleration and Deceleration:**

Smooth acceleration through impact and controlled deceleration.

1. Impact:

Contact with the ball at the sweet spot of the putter.

1. Follow-through:

Smooth continuation of the stroke after impact, maintaining direction.

1. Distance Control:

Adjusting length of stroke for different putt distances.

1. Putter Face Angle:

Maintaining square alignment of the putter face at impact.

1. Reading Greens:

Assessing slopes and breaks to aim the putt correctly.

These aspects highlight the complexity and precision involved in both the full golf swing and the putting stroke, each requiring attention to detail and practice to master.

3. Golf Game/Course Management

Golf course management involves strategic decision-making to navigate the course effectively and optimize your scoring opportunities. It encompasses different aspects across the long game, middle game, and short game. Here's how each aspect breaks down:

Long Game Management:

1. **Club Selection:**

    Choosing the appropriate club based on distance, wind conditions, and hazards.

1. **Shot Shape:**

    Deciding whether to hit a draw, fade, or straight shot to avoid trouble and position for the next shot.

1. **Course Strategy:**

    Planning the sequence of shots to play to set up for optimal approach shots to greens.

1. **Tee Shot Placement:**

    Positioning tee shots to provide the best angle for the next shot into the green.

1. Risk vs. Reward:

Assessing whether to go for a more aggressive shot or play it safe based on the potential rewards and risks.

Middle Game Management:

1. Approach Shot Strategy:

Selecting the appropriate club and aiming for the correct portion of the green to avoid hazards and set up for a manageable putt.

1. Green Reading:

Analyzing the contours, slopes, and speed of the green to determine the line and speed of the putt.

1. Layup Shots:

Strategically placing shots short of hazards or at a specific distance to set up for a better approach or pitch shot.

1. Recovery Shots:

Choosing the best shot to recover from trouble (e.g., rough, bunker) while minimizing strokes.

Short Game Management:

1. **Chipping/Pitching Strategy:**

Assessing lie and green conditions to decide on the type of shot and landing area to get close to the hole.

1. **Bunker Play:**

Choosing the appropriate club and technique to get out of bunkers and onto the green or near the hole.

1. **Putting Strategy:**

Planning the line, speed, and break of putts to give the best chance for holing out or leaving a tap-in.

1. **Distance Control:**

Controlling the distance of chips, pitches, and putts to leave manageable second putts or avoid three-putting.

1. **Course Conditions Awareness:**

Adapting strategies based on course conditions such as green firmness, wind direction, and pin placements.

Effective golf course management involves integrating these aspects seamlessly throughout a round to maximize scoring opportunities while minimizing errors and penalties. It requires knowledge of one's own strengths and weaknesses, as well as a thorough understanding of the course layout and conditions.

When you're with someone who is sharing their struggles with you...just smile at him/her and give them one of these. He/she will ask "What is that?" Then simply reply "Life Works in Threes."

Other titles coming out:

- Weight Struggles?
- Abundance Struggles?
- Parenting Struggles?
- Life Struggles?
- Purpose Struggles?
- Happiness Struggles?
- Sales Struggles?
- Speaker Struggles?
- Time Struggles?
- Network Struggles?
- Marriage Struggles?
- Divorce Struggles?
- Money Struggles?
- Career Struggles?
- Dating Struggles?
- Caretaker Struggles?
- Forgiveness Struggles?
- Grieving Struggles?
- Success Struggles?
- Romance Struggles?
- Workplace Struggles?
- Stress Struggles?
- Shame/Guilt Struggles?
- Addiction Struggles?

Quotes about Golf

"Golf is a game in which you yell 'fore,' shoot six, and write down five." - Paul Harvey

"Golf is deceptively simple and endlessly complicated." - Arnold Palmer

"There's two things that don't last: dogs chasing cars and pros putting for pars."

- Lee Trevino

"Golf is like a love affair. If you don't take it seriously, it's no fun; if you do take it seriously, it breaks your heart." - Arthur Daley

"Golf is the most fun you can have without taking your clothes off." - Chi Chi Rodriguez

When someone is struggling with a particular area or two, chances are they are "out of balance" with how life works. How does life work? Life works in threes.

If you're interested in personal topics like life, health, money or business topics like sales, time management and public speaking...Life Works in Threes! can shed some light on creating success in those areas.

The definition of TRIUNE is a group of three things; united. Being three in one, such as - humans are *mental, physical* and *spiritual beings.* The word TRYUNE is a play of the word TRIUNE, encouraging all to try this concept and help eliminate struggling unnecessarily.

LifeWorksInThrees.com